Back Tested Moving Average Systems for Trend Traders QQQ Exchange

By Steve Burns & Holly Burns

Contents

Disclaimer

This book is meant to be informational and shouldn't be used as trading or investing advice. All readers should gather information from multiple sources to create their personalized investment strategies and trading systems. The authors make no guarantees related to the claims contained herein. Always seek the advice of a competent licensed professional before implementing any plan or system that involves your money. Please invest and trade responsibly.

Foreword

"If you diversify, control your risk, and go with the trend, it just has to work." – Larry Hite

Have you been frustrated by not knowing when to get in and out of the stock market? This book will show you how to overcome this frustration and up your trading game.

This book is based on my own learning curve, as I experienced heavy losses during the Dot Com meltdown. After years of investing and trading in the tech sector in the 90's, by March of 2000 my investment account was enough to pay off my house. But by the time I reached my maximum drawdown in early 2003, that same account was down 50% from my earlier equity highs. My large losses gave me an aversion to risk and losing money, and prompted me to learn a better way to make more money with less risks.

This book explains strategies to trade price action to lock in profits. The back tests in this book show what you could have done after the year 2000, to lock in your gains from the late 1990's when the NASDAQ went from 750-

5000, before the crash took the $QQQ exchange traded fund down by 83%. This book gives is designed to give you quantified signals on how to get in when there is a potential for gains, and when to get out when there is a chance that the market could go into a correction or crash.

This book is a map that shows you how to navigate your tech holdings through market booms and busts, so you can grow your capital and limit your losses. I use the principles in this book in my own trading, and I hope these quantified examples will help you know when to get in and out of your stock positions when a trend starts, stops, ends, or bends.

Why Trade the $QQQ Exchange Traded Fund?

"Take your profits or someone else will take them for you." – J.J. Evans

An exchange traded fund (ETF), is a security that can be traded on a stock exchange intra-day that tracks an index, a commodity, bonds, or a specific sector. Some ETFs can also add leverage to what it is tracking with 2X or 3X the daily movement of the underlying. Mutual funds can only be traded at the end of the day but an ETF trades like a stock all day from open until close. ETFs have real-time quotes through the entire trading day as they are bought and sold. Mutual funds only have end of day price quotes. They flexibility of trading an ETF is much better than the limitations of a Mutual fund.

This book will be using the PowerShares™ QQQ exchange traded fund for all the charts and back testing for potential trading systems. The QQQ ticker is an ETF that trades on the NASDAQ like a stock and attempts to track the daily movement of the NASDAQ 100 Index. The QQQ tracks

100 of the largest international and domestic companies, excluding financial companies that are listed on the NASDAQ market, based on the size of the market capitalization. The QQQ will at any time consist of about 100 stocks in the NASDAQ 100 index. (There can be more than 100 stocks in this index).

The current stocks in the NASDAQ 100 index as of this writing are:

ADBE-Adobe Systems Inc

ADI-Analog Devices Inc

ADP-Automatic Data Processing Inc

ADSK-Autodesk Inc

AKAM-Akamai Technologies Inc

ALXN-Alexion Pharmaceuticals Inc

AMAT-Applied Materials Inc

AMGN-Amgen Inc

AMZN-Amazon.com Inc

ATVI-Activision Blizzard Inc

AVGO-Broadcom Ltd

BIDU-Baidu Inc

BIIB-Biogen Inc

BMRN-Biomarin Pharmaceutical Inc

CA-CA Inc

CELG-Celgene Corp

CERN-Cerner Corp

CHKP-Check Point Software Technologies Ltd

CHTR-Charter Communications Inc

CTRP-Ctrip.Com International Ltd

CTAS-Cintas Corp

CSCO-Cisco Systems Inc

CTXS-Citrix Systems Inc

CMCSA-Comcast Corp

COST-Costco Wholesale Corp

CSX-CSX Corp

CTSH-Cognizant Technology Solutions Corp

DISCA-Discovery Communications Inc

DISCK-Discovery Communications Inc

DISH-DISH Network Corp

DLTR-Dollar Tree Inc

EA-Electronic Arts

EBAY-eBay Inc

ESRX-Express Scripts Holding Co

EXPE-Expedia Inc

FAST-Fastenal Co

FB-Facebook

FISV-Fiserv Inc

FOX-21st Century Fox Class B

FOXA-21st Century Fox Class A

GILD-Gilead Sciences Inc

GOOG-Alphabet Class C

GOOGL-Alphabet Class A

HAS-Hasbro Inc

HSIC-Henry Schein Inc

HOLX-Hologic Inc

ILMN-Illumina Inc

INCY-Incyte Corp

INTC-Intel Corp

INTU-Intuit Inc

ISRG-Intuitive Surgical Inc

JBHT-J.B. Hunt Transport Services Inc

JD-JD.com Inc

KLAC-KLA-Tencor Corp

KHC-Kraft Heinz Co

LBTYA-Liberty Global PLC

LBTYK-Liberty Global PLC

LILA-Liberty Global PLC

LILAK-Liberty Global PLC

LRCX-Lam Research Corp

QVCA-Liberty Interactive Corp

LVNTA-Liberty Interactive Corp

MAR-Marriott International Inc

MAT-Mattel Inc

MCHP-Microchip Technology Inc

MDLZ-Mondelez International Inc

MNST-Monster Beverage Corp

MSFT-Microsoft Corp

MU-Micron Technology Inc

MXIM-Maxim Integrated Products Inc

MYL-Mylan NV

NCLH-Norwegian Cruise Line Holdings Ltd

NFLX-Netflix Inc

NTES-NetEase Inc

NVDA-NVIDIA Corp

ORLY-O'Reilly Automotive Inc

PAYX-Paychex Inc

PCAR-PACCAR Inc

PCLN-The Priceline Group

PYPL-PayPal Holdings Inc

QCOM-Qualcomm Inc

REGN-Regeneron Pharmaceuticals Inc

ROST-Ross Stores Inc

SBAC-SBA Communications Corp

STX-Seagate Technology PLC

SHPG-Shire PLC

SIRI-Sirius XM Holdings Inc

SWKS-Skyworks Solutions Inc

SBUX-Starbucks Corp

SYMC-Symantec Corp

TMUS-T-Mobile US Inc

TRIP-TripAdvisor Inc

TSCO-Tractor Supply Co

TSLA-Tesla Inc

TXN-Texas Instruments Inc

ULTA-Ulta Beauty Inc

VIAB-Viacom Inc

VOD-Vodafone Group PLC

VRSK-Verisk Analytics Inc

VRTX-Vertex Pharmaceuticals Inc

WBA-Walgreens Boots Alliance Inc

WDC-Western Digital Corp

XLNX-Xilinx Inc

XRAY-Dentsply Sirona Inc

YHOO-Yahoo Inc

The QQQ is a tracking ETF of the NASDAQ-100 index.
The NADAQ 100 currently consists of 107 stocks of the
100 largest non-financial companies that are listed on the
NASDAQ stock exchange. The NASDAQ 100 is a
modified capitalization-weighted index. The stocks'

weighting in the index is based on their own market capitalizations. Unlike other stock market indexes, the NASDAQ 100 has rules capping the influence of the largest components on the price movement of the total index. It is based on stocks that trade on the NASDAQ stock exchange. This is not an index of U.S.-based companies. The NASDAQ 100 has no financial sector companies in it since they are in a separate index, the NASDAQ Financial 100. The NASDAQ 100 contains Industrial, Technology, Retail, Telecommunication, Biotechnology, Health Care, Transportation, Media, and Service companies. The NASDAQ Financial 100 consists of banking companies, insurance firms, brokerage houses and mortgage companies. The NASDAQ-100 is often confused with the NASADQ Composite Index; the complete NASDAQ composite index is commonly referred to as *"The NASDAQ"* on financial news. The NASDAQ composite index includes the stock of every company that is listed on the NASDAQ stock exchange (more than 3,000 altogether) and is quoted more frequently than the NASDAQ 100 in popular media. (Source: Wikipedia)

Here are the current NASDAQ 100 Sector Weightings at the time of publication:

Consumer Goods – 5.3%

Consumer Services – 24.41%

Health Care – 10.94%

Industrials – 4.21%

Technology –54.07 %

Telecommunications –1.04 %

As you can see this is a heavily weighted tech index with over half the index consisting of tech companies that are traded on the NASDAQ stock exchange. This index has no financial sector exposure so it should outperform the other indexes when the financial sector is in a downtrend and tech is in favor. This index carries heavy tech exposure but also diversification that helps smooth out the total risk of hot technology stocks during bubbles with 45% diversification it has in other sectors. The QQQ ETF was a great vehicle to use to ride the Dot Com uptrend up from 1995-2000 if you took your exit from moving averages when the trend started to reverse and lose all support levels in price. Using this more diversified ETF is one way to get exposure to the tech sector while using moving average stop losses to cap the downside. I believe that the QQQ ETF is a good trading and investing vehicle for those that understand the risks and have quantified entry and exit plans in place based on a quantified and back tested system that is historically profitable. This book will be showing back tested signals for getting in and out of the QQQ ETF for maximum profits and minimum losses during uptrends, downtrends, bubbles, crashes, and meltdowns. The QQQ ETF experienced bubbles, bull markets, corrections, and crashes during the period of the back tests you will see from 2000-2017.

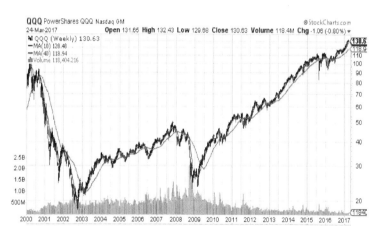

This Chart is Courtesy of StockCharts.com

From January 3, 2000 to March 24, 2017 QQQ returned 53.4% with an 83% drawdown. (Data courtesy of ETFreplay.com)

Does buy and hold investing work? It depends on the year you buy, what period of years you add to your investment, and when your capital peaks in value and you start to withdraw. For someone near retirement in the year 2000 or 2007 with a large account heavily exposed to the stock market it was financially, mentally, and emotionally tough to watch your account meltdown while being reassured everything would be fine. If you were in the NASDAQ 100 it was not fine to lose over 80% of your accounts value due to no exit plan to lock in profits or if the pain made you exit then the danger of having no plan on entry to enter with a great margin of safety once the market did begin to recovery. This book is not created to show these signals in the best possible way, 1990-2000 would have been a better back testing period. I also showed the tough period from 2000- March 2017 that was very flat from a trend following perspective instead of back testing from the 2002 or 2009 bottom to the new all-time high. These are common moving averages used that I have tested in other ETFs so they are not data mining. These back tests are what they show with the primary goal of simply doing what so many think is impossible, beating the market and beating the cult of buy and hold. I know it is possible to beat the market and buy and hold in both returns and drawdowns because I did these things myself over long periods of time in many of the last 20 years and plan to continue to do so.

From the bubble price peak high of March 2000 QQQ lost 83% of its value and would not bring buy and hold investors back to even in price until 2015. Trend following with moving average systems can do much better than buy and hold investing. While buy and hold is looked at as a religion by many personal financial advisors and in the mutual fund industry the QQQ chart above shows the true dangers of simply buying and hoping instead of having a systematic process for entries and exits that allow you to capture trends. A profitable stock market system simply means having a strategy to be long during bull markets and out during bear markets. It is crucial when you have an opportunity to lock in gains that you have a plan to do so. The skill of buying and holding with discipline can make you money but it can also lead to you giving back all that money. The real pain of losing so much paper profits during 2000-2002 and then again in 2008 can 't be expressed with the above chart. Seeing and feeling a $100,000 account turn into a $17,000 account is what many people experienced from 2000-2002. Some people that were near retirement and heavy in tech stocks saw $1,000,000 turn into $170,000. It was better for people that had more diversification in other big cap indexes but even worse for people that had bought individual Dot Com bubble stocks and rode them all the way down. So, we have identified the problem and what happened, now let's look at a different way to beat the market.

Introduction to Using Moving Averages as Reactive Technical Indicators

"Most of this trend following "science" can be explained by a decent moving average crossover. Don't over-indulge in complexity." - Jerry Parker

~Moving averages can be used to quantify trends in price on different time frames.

~Price moving through a moving average can be used as a signal for entries and exits.

~Unlike trend lines and chart patterns, moving averages can be quantified.

~Moving average crossover systems are a way to capture trends by entering a trade when a shorter moving average crosses over a longer term one, then exiting as it crosses back under.

~Moving average crossover systems are a way to trade based on price trends instead of personal opinions or fundamentals.

~A moving average crossover signal can keep you on the right side of a market trend.

~In the short-term, a moving average crossover system will give fewer signals than a moving average being used alone. This can help filter out volatility.

~Moving average crossover systems can be back tested in different market environments using web based tools.

~The longer the time frame, the less entries and exits you will have to take.

~Moving average signals can beat buy and hold investing because they let winning trades run. They also give exit signals to lock in profits and help you exit losing trades early.

There are several ways to use moving averages as technical indicators in your trading and investing. The first way is to incorporate them as a trend filter in your trading system. They can also be used as standalone signals, allowing you to buy a stock or index when the price rises above a long-term moving average like the 200-day simple moving average, and exit when price falls back under the 200-day simple moving average. Another way to use moving averages in a trading system is by using two moving averages that give buy and sell signals when a shorter moving average crosses over a longer one.

Legendary trend trading pioneer Richard Donchian used a five and twenty day moving average crossover system along with some other filters for entry and exit signals. Donchian was a pioneer in trading based on reacting to technical price action. He was one of the first modern day quantitative trend followers that used mechanical trend trading systems instead of forecasts, opinions, and predictions. Other traders known for embracing quantitative trading in their own entries and exits were Jesse Livermore, Nicolas Darvas, and Ed Seykota.

The best way to smooth out entries and exits during more volatile market periods is to develop trading systems using moving average crossovers. Using two moving averages, you can create entry signals that are triggered when the shorter moving average crosses over the longer term moving average. The exit signal is triggered when the shorter moving average crosses back underneath the longer term moving average.

Your trading time frame and back tests determine which moving average best suits your trading vehicle, time frame, and methodology. Short-term moving averages that are two quick to trigger an entry signal can generate false signals before catching a trend. Many moving averages that are too short-term are unprofitable to trade because they generate losses during volatile markets. Short-term moving average signals generate more signals than systems with long-term moving averages. In this book, we will be testing the performance of different lengths of moving averages that may fit your own trading time frame and holding time preferences, helping you achieve better results.

Long-term moving average crossover systems can give back some open paper profits before the exit is triggered, because price must move down drastically to trigger the sell signal. However, a long-term moving average's strength is in keeping you long for the duration of a long-term bull market, like we witnessed in the NASDAQ from 1995-1999. The underlying principle is that you develop a moving average crossover system that enables you to have big wins and small losses. The purpose of moving average crossover systems is to replace opinions and predictions with a quantifiable way to capture trends. A great moving average signal will capture both momentum near a break out to higher prices, and it will get you long after a price bottom when price finally starts to trend up again. The systems in this book are all long-only systems from 2000 to 2017. The selling short side trend signals struggled after a few years and weren't shown to be winning systems. Therefore, they haven't been included in this book.

A moving average crossover system waits for a confirmation of a trend and forces the trader to act based on what is happening with the price trend, and not their own personal perceptions. The short-term moving average is the signal line, and your long-term moving average is your trend filter. This gives you an edge over most traders that are trading from their gut. The best predictor of a future trend is the present trend going in the direction of least resistance, until it stops.

Moving average crossover systems can decrease the amount of trades and losses as opposed to using one short-term moving average signal alone. A single long-term moving average system can beat buy and hold, but the signal can be rare and you must wait for it; sometimes for months or even a year. With single moving averages, price may penetrate and go through a key moving average several times before trending in one direction. This can cause multiple losses. In contrast, a crossover system may only have one entry and one exit in the same time frame. By using moving average crossover systems as opposed to a single moving average, the quality and frequency of your signals increase, and false signals decrease.

About the Moving Average Systems in This Book

In a mechanical system, you must trade the technical signals exactly how they are back tested to increase potential profits and avoid discretionary decisions.

Unlike short-term single moving averages that rarely work as standalone technical indicators in varied market environments, moving average crossover systems can be standalone trading systems that can outperform market returns, and beat buy and hold investing in the long-term.

These are back tested systems not forward tested. While the principles of the systems are sound for capturing trends in the past, the future can be very different. The systems are designed to let winners run and cut losses short. With these signals, you could be in cash during most of the large market downtrends, and be long during strong bull markets.

Here are some popular moving average crossovers that are back tested in this book. Choose the ones that match your time frame.

~ 5-day EMA/20-day EMA crossover

~ 10-day EMA/50-day EMA crossover

~ 10-day EMA/100-day EMA crossover

~ 50-day EMA/100-day EMA crossover

~ 10-day EMA/200-day EMA crossover

~ Price crossing the 200-day EMA

~ Price crossing the 250-day SMA

Here is an example of how the 10-day EMA/50-day EMA crossover signal can be used to increase returns and decrease drawdowns in markets with wide price swings. By going long when the 10-day EMA crosses over the 50-day EMA, and exiting the long when the 10-day EMA goes back under the 50-day EMA, a trader can capture the upswings in a strongly trending market. The key to using this model is making sure that your wins are large and your losing trades are small. You can catch uptrends and maximize gains in a bull market by staying on one side of a trending chart for long periods.

Chart Courtesy of StockCharts.com

While studying charts and back testing past data for moving average crossover systems, it's necessary that you test and view data in different market environments. A long only system that works great in bull markets may be unprofitable in bear markets, or may take you to cash at the beginning of a downtrend. While the long side of the crossover may result in losses during bear market rallies, it can result in large wins when the market finds a bottom and begins a new uptrend.

After a correction or bear market, moving average crossover long signals have the potential for a great risk/return entry price level. The best signals for many of these systems will look dangerous in real-time, because you are buying a strong rally after a downtrend, or a near term breakout in price. You must commit to following a mechanical trading system and stick to your plan to make a moving average system work long-term. Be flexible in your opinion of where the market price may go, but be disciplined with your system and trading rules.

It is also important to trade a position size that allows you to manage your emotions if markets move against you in the short-term. The QQQ chart below shows that a 10-day EMA/50-day EMA crossover system alone would have taken a long only strategy to cash before the 2000-2002 market bubble popped, thereby avoiding the meltdown. Moving average crossover systems can keep you from large losses and drawdowns during strong, sustained parabolic downtrends. However, these plunges are rare and generally only happen once a decade. A long only moving average crossover system will generally keep you safe and in cash when these plunges occur.

The exit was here as the 10 day EMA crossed under the 50 day EMA.

No entry crossover signal here

There was no entry signal for the length of this chart.

Chart Courtesy of StockCharts.com

Many system traders abandon good trading systems during bad market environments. Don't abandon good long-term trading systems based on bad short-term results. Moving average crossover systems that rely on uptrends to be profitable will have losses in tight, rangebound or volatile markets. The key is to keep the losses small and take the next entry for a chance to capture a winner. Keep drawdowns small by trading a position size that limits your total trading capital risk exposure. You can trade larger position sizes with stock index ETFs and the drawdowns of the systems in this book are reasonable for the potential returns.

The below QQQ chart would have been in real-time, as 2015 became a tightly rangebound market and paper profits vanished. The good thing about this 10-day/50-day EMA cross as a standalone system, is that it limited the quantity of losing trades, saving commission costs and keeping a good winning percentage. This is another advantage to making trading decisions at the end of the day; you avoid the intra-day noise. This system also does a good job of getting out before the crash days, and then getting back in before the gap up and price recovery. This limited the drawdown in capital, maximized the profits with a fast re-entry, and saved the trader emotional stress.

Chart Courtesy of StockCharts.com

Profitable long only moving average crossover systems used for individual stocks and stock indices can reduce drawdowns in capital during bear markets. Many long-term systems can decrease drawdowns by 50% and outperform buy and hold investing over long periods of time.

Moving average crossover systems that reverse and sell short can be profitable in bear markets, but can underperform long-term, because the stock market spends most of its time in bull markets.

I advise a mechanical back test of any moving average trading system before live trading to test your system's potential. Adjustments should be made during the trading system's development phase and not after the the market price action influences you.

Moving average crossover systems can be profitable long-term, but they can produce an uncomfortable equity curve in real-time trading, depending on the trader's expectations and the market volatility. It takes time and uptrends for these systems to be profitable in the long-term.

Summary:

~A moving crossover system is when a short-term moving average crosses over a longer term one and is then exited, going to a cash position when it crosses back over from the other direction.

~Moving average crossover systems are typically used as a mechanical trading methods for trading a market through price action. These systems are mechanical to insure consistent performance. Mechanical systems can remove the stress and emotions in a trader's decision-making process. It takes discipline to follow a mechanical trading.

~Using a short-term moving average crossover system instead of a single short-term moving average alone lowers the quantity of your trades, increasing your chance of capturing a longer trend while lowering commission costs and churn rate.

~Mechanical moving average crossover systems can be back tested for historical performance.

~Moving averages crossover systems can filter out the noise in a chart and provide quantifiable signals.

5-day/20-day Exponential Moving Average Crossover System

This is one of the original moving averages used in Richard Donchian's first trend following systems for commodities. He had more parameters for using these two moving averages in a trend following system, but adapting these as a crossover system beat buy and hold investors in QQQ.

This short-term system doubled the return of only holding the QQQ ETF from March 2000 to 2017, and it also cut the drawdown in capital by half. This is an active system that can create good returns in some years, but can have flat returns on an annualized basis when the market doesn't have a swing up in price or trend. Over the long-term, this system can double your money, even during bubbles like the Dot Com collapse and the financial crisis. This system gets you in and out fast. You need big up swings in price to benefit from this system in the short-term. You will enjoy a high winning percentage with this system.

Here are the variables that this platform uses to help understand any variance against other back testing sites or software. These were my settings.

~Dividends are included in the back tests.

~You will enter this system on the first day that the 5-day EMA crosses back over the 20-day EMA. The following back tests are based on the first cross. Back test will wait until the ETF crosses above the moving average before making the first buy. This system waits for an end of day trend signal to enter after a 5-day/20-day EMA crossover. This is not a system to enter immediately, because the results will be skewed with an initial bad risk/reward entry at elevated price levels if the moving averages are already crossed.

~This system's signals are taken at the end of the day, the day of the actual moving average crossover. This is the daily chart timeframe. The system only looks to enter or exit at the end of the day based on whether the 5-day EMA is over or under the 20-day EMA. It only gives a signal at this crossover, and this system can go weeks and months with no entry or exit signals. You will be in cash when the 5-day EMA is below the 20-day EMA, and long when the 5-day EMA is above the 20-day EMA.

~This is a moving average crossover system and not the standard moving average system.

~You are trading a moving average crossing another moving average instead of price crossing a moving average.

~This system will keep you long through short-term up swings in the market.

~This system will most likely take you to cash quickly as a market swings downward in price in the short-term.

~This system helps you avoid downturns in the market due to its fast signals.

~This system uses the 5-day exponential moving average and the 20-day exponential moving average. This 5-day and 20-day moving averages of prices is based on the total return data series that includes dividends and distributions with more weight given to the more current prices.

~The 5-day exponential moving average is the average of 5 daily total return values with more weight given to the more current prices

~The 20-day exponential moving average is the average of 20 daily total return values with more weight given to the more current prices.

~This system attempts to take short-term swing trades to the long side and exit as the market goes sideways or starts to swing downward. However, this option helps short-term performance by reducing the time frame of the long-term moving average signal. This reduces the wait time for price to move all the way back to the 250-day EMA, or to the 200-day.

~This system gets you out fast to lock in short-term profits. It closes paper profits quickly at the first sign of a downturn.

~This system will also get you back in quick if the market rallies strong on the daily chart.

~This is an active system. You must watch every day for a 5-day/20-day EMA moving average cross. In a very volatile market, you could get signals to enter and then exit on back to back days, getting caught up in a lot of noise.

~This system gives you faster long-term moving average lines than any other systems in this book. It can be used by swing traders or traders that don't like to hold for long periods of time, or who hate to give back open profits as a market pulls back, corrects, or goes into a bear market.

How did the 5-day EMA/20-day EMA Crossover System perform?

Chart Courtesy of ETFreplay.com

Historical 16 year backtest				
Backtest period	January 3rd 2000 to March 24th 2017			
Backtest Parameters		**5 day/20 day EMA crossvoer**		

Winning Trades	Losing Trades		Median Win	Median Loss
65.9%	34.1%		5.32%	-2.10%

Maximum Consecutive Trades			Average Days in a Trade	
Wins	Losses		Wins	Losses
3	8		43	9

Max Drawdown			Return percentage	
Backtest	$QQQ		Backtest	$QQQ
-38.9%	-83.0%		102.4%	57.8%

Historical backtest in a sideways market				
Backtest period	March 24 2000 to June 18 2015			
Backtest Parameters		**5 day/20 day EMA crossvoer**		

Winning Trades	Losing Trades		Median Win	Median Loss
66.7%	33.3%		4.77%	-2.14%

Maximum Consecutive Trades			Average Days in a Trade	
Wins	Losses		Wins	Losses
3	8		43	9

Max Drawdown			Return percentage	
Backtest	$QQQ		Backtest	$QQQ
-35.7%	-83.0%		64.3%	28.8%

Historical backtest from a market top to a market bottom				
Backtest period	March 24 2000 to October 10 2002			
Backtest Parameters		**5 day/20 day EMA crossvoer**		

Winning Trades	Losing Trades		Median Win	Median Loss
7.7%	92.3%		11.79%	-3.33%

Maximum Consecutive Trades			Average Days in a Trade	
Wins	Losses		Wins	Losses
1	8		49	12

Max Drawdown			Return percentage	
Backtest	$QQQ		Backtest	$QQQ
35.7%	-83.0%		-29.1%	-77.5%

Back test data courtesy of ETFreplay.com

The 10-day/ 50-day Exponential Moving Average Crossover System

The 10-day/50-day crossover tests well across several markets. It cut drawdowns in half compared to buy and hold, and doubled the return of the QQQ ETF. This system can trigger entries that are held for months to keep you on the right side of a long-term uptrend. It is less vulnerable to volatility than the 5-day /20-day crossover, so it has less drawdown. This closely tracks the return of the ETF when it's in a strong uptrend, but gets you out faster than other long-term moving averages. The main reason this system beat the ETF is because the drawdowns were much smaller. This provides a smoother equity curve than some of the other systems. The returns aren't impressive annualized, but the individual losses aren't large, and drawdown is almost one-third of buy and hold on the QQQ ETF for the timeframes tested.

Here are the variables that this platform uses to help understand any variance against other back testing sites or software. These were my settings.

~Dividends are included in the back tests.

~You will enter this system on the first day that the 10-day EMA crosses back over the 50-day EMA. The following back tests are based on the first cross. Back test will wait until the ETF crosses above the moving average before making the first buy. This system waits for a better trend signal to enter after a 10-day/50-day EMA crossover. This is not a system to enter immediately as the results will be skewed with an initial bad risk/reward entry at elevated levels if the moving averages are already crossed.

~This system's signals are taken at the end of the day, the day of the actual moving average crossover. This is the daily chart timeframe and it is a long-term system. It only looks to enter or exit at the end of the day based on whether the 10-day EMA is over or under the 50-day EMA. It only gives a signal at this crossover, and this system can go weeks and months with no entry or exit signals. You will be in cash when the 10-day EMA is below the 50-day ~EMA, and long when the 10-day EMA is above the 50-day EMA.

~This is a moving average crossover system and not the standard moving average system.

~You are trading a moving average crossing another moving average instead of price crossing a moving average.

~This system will help keep you long through most of the strong bull markets.

~This system will likely take you to cash as a market starts to trend downward.

~This system allows you to avoid large pullbacks, bear markets, and crashes.

~This system uses the 10-day exponential moving average and the 50-day exponential moving average. This 10-day and 50-day moving averages of prices is based on the total return data series that includes dividends and distributions, with more weight given to the more current prices.

~The 10-day exponential moving average is the average of 10 daily total return values with more weight given to the more current prices.

~The 50-day exponential moving average is the average of 50 daily total return values with more weight given to the more current prices.

~This system is taking a signal only when the 10-day EMA moves through the 50-day EMA on the daily timeframe. This system attempts to balance the risk of giving back capital gains during a bull market, with staying long when an uptrend is confirmed. However, this option helps performance in the short-term by reducing the time frame of the long-term moving average signal to reduce the wait time for the 50-day EMA to move all the way back to the 100-day.

~This system gets you out faster daily than the other long-term systems in this book, such as the 250-day SMA or the 200-day EMA price crossover. This helps you avoid any fast moves to the downside.

~This system can get you back in quicker if the market rallies strong on the daily chart, versus the 250-day EMA or a 200-day EMA alone.

~This can be a more active system. You must watch for a 10-day/ 50-day moving average crossover, daily.

~This system gives you a faster long-term moving average line to trigger an entry than the other long-term moving average crossovers that you will see next in this book. This system has quicker entries and quicker exits to lock in profits.

How would the 10-day EMA/50-day EMA Crossover System perform?

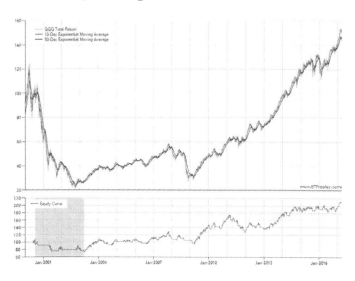

Chart Courtesy of ETFreplay.com

Historical 16 year backtest				
Backtest period	January 3rd 2000 to March 24th 2017			
Backtest Parameters			**10 day/50 day EMA crossvoer**	

Winning Trades	Losing Trades		Median Win	Median Loss
57.1%	42.9%		5.20%	-3.58%

Maximum Consecutive Trades			Average Days in a Trade	
Wins	Losses		Wins	Losses
4	6		95	14

Max Drawdown			Return percentage	
Backtest	$QQQ		Backtest	$QQQ
-33.8%	-83.0%		110.1%	54.2%

Historical backtest in a sideways market				
Backtest period	March 24 2000 to June 18 2015			
Backtest Parameters			**10 day/50 day EMA crossvoer**	

Winning Trades	Losing Trades		Median Win	Median Loss
40.0%	60.0%		6.41%	-3.58%

Maximum Consecutive Trades			Average Days in a Trade	
Wins	Losses		Wins	Losses
4	6		100	13

Max Drawdown			Return percentage	
Backtest	$QQQ		Backtest	$QQQ
-33.8%	-83.0%		97.4%	28.0%

Historical backtest from a market top to a market bottom				
Backtest period	March 24 2000 to October 10 2002			
Backtest Parameters			**10 day/50 day EMA crossvoer**	

Winning Trades	Losing Trades		Median Win	Median Loss
16.7%	83.3%		4.54%	-5.10%

Maximum Consecutive Trades			Average Days in a Trade	
Wins	Losses		Wins	Losses
1	5		53	15

Max Drawdown			Return percentage	
Backtest	$QQQ		Backtest	$QQQ
-30.2%	-83.0%		-21.2%	-77.6%

Back test data courtesy of ETFreplay.com

The 10-day/100-day Exponential Moving Average Crossover System

This system did well with drawdowns in sideways markets, and better in downtrends because it avoided a lot of false signals caused by volatility. This is a slower system that gets in and out later than the previous systems. This system has fewer signals and avoids a lot price noise, but it is slower getting in and out of trends. This system has a lower winning percent than the other two systems, but holds longer once in a trend. You can capture longer trends with this system, and the returns cut drawdowns in half and almost doubled returns compared to buying and holding the QQQ ETF.

Here are the variables that this platform uses to help understand any variance against other back testing sites or software. These were my settings.

~Dividends are included in the back tests.
~You will enter this system on the first day that the 10-day EMA crosses back over the 100-day EMA. The following back tests are based on the first cross. Back test will wait until the shorter moving average crosses above the long-term moving average before making the first buy. This

system waits for a better trend signal to enter after a 10-day/100-day EMA crossover. This is not a system to enter immediately, because the results will be skewed with an initial bad risk/reward entry at elevated levels if the moving averages are already crossed.

~This system's signals are taken at the end of the day, the day of the actual moving average crossover. This is the daily chart timeframe and it is a long-term system, only looking to enter or exit at the end of the day based on whether the 10-day EMA is over or under the 100-day EMA. It only gives a signal at this crossover, and this system can go weeks and months with no entry or exit signals. You will be in cash when the 10-day EMA is below the 100-day ~EMA and long when the 10-day EMA is above the 100-day EMA.

~This is a moving average crossover system not the standard moving average system.

~You are trading a moving average crossing another moving average instead of price crossing a moving average.

~This system will help keep you long through most of the strong bull markets.

~This system will likely take you to cash as a market starts to trend downward.

~This system helps you avoid pullbacks, bear markets, and crashes.

~This system uses the 10-day exponential moving average and the 100-day exponential moving average. This 10-day and 100-day moving averages of prices is based on the total return data series that includes dividends and distributions, with more weight given to the more current prices.

~The 10-day exponential moving average is the average of 10 daily total return values with more weight given to the more current prices.

~The 100-day exponential moving average is the average of 100 daily total return values with more weight given to the more current prices.

~This system takes a signal only when the 10-day EMA moves through the 100-day EMA on the daily timeframe. This system attempts to balance the risk of giving back capital gains during a bull market, with staying long when an uptrend is confirmed. However, this option helps performance by reducing the time frame of the long-term moving average signal, reducing the wait time for exits and entries.

~This system can get you out faster than the 250-day SMA alone or the 200-day EMA system daily.

~This system can get you back in quicker if the market rallies strong on the daily chart versus the 250-day EMA or a 200-day EMA alone.

~This can be a more active system, and you must watch for a 10-day/100-day moving average cross daily.

~This system gives you a faster long-term moving average line versus the 200-day EMA. This system should have quicker exits to lock in profits and quicker entries over the long-term.

How would the 10-day EMA/100-day EMA Crossover System perform?

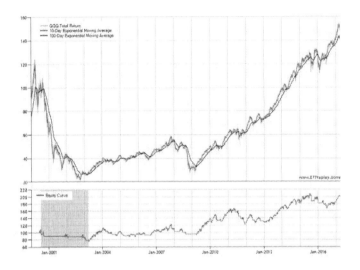

Chart Courtesy of ETFreplay.com

Historical 16 year backtest				
Backtest period	January 3rd 2000 to March 24th 2017			
Backtest Parameters		**10 day/100 day EMA price crossover**		

Winning Trades	Losing Trades		Median Win	Median Loss
36.8%	63.2%		8.01%	-3.90%

Maximum Consecutive Trades			Average Days in a Trade	
Wins	Losses		Wins	Losses
4	5		161	25

Max Drawdown			Return percentage	
Backtest	$QQQ		Backtest	$QQQ
33.0%	83.0%		101.7%	57.8%

Historical backtest in a sideways market				
Backtest period	March 24 2000 to June 18 2015			
Backtest Parameters		**10 day/100 day EMA price crossover**		

Winning Trades	Losing Trades		Median Win	Median Loss
38.2%	61.8%		9.10%	-4.20%

Maximum Consecutive Trades			Average Days in a Trade	
Wins	Losses		Wins	Losses
4	5		156	23

Max Drawdown			Return percentage	
Backtest	$QQQ		Backtest	$QQQ
-33.0%	-83.0%		102.0%	30.9%

Historical backtest from a market top to a market bottom				
Backtest period	March 24 2000 to October 10 2002			
Backtest Parameters		**10 day/100 day EMA price crossover**		

Winning Trades	Losing Trades		Median Win	Median Loss
0.0%	100.0%		0.00%	-4.20%

Maximum Consecutive Trades			Average Days in a Trade	
Wins	Losses		Wins	Losses
0	3		0	33

Max Drawdown			Return percentage	
Backtest	$QQQ		Backtest	$QQQ
-22.9%	-83.0%		-11.3%	-77.1%

Back test data courtesy of ETFreplay.com

The 50-day/100-day Exponential Moving Average Crossover System

This system tripled the returns and cut the drawdown in half compared to holding the QQQ ETF through all market environments. This is a good system for capturing trends and avoiding noise. The winning percent is over 50%, which is good for a trend following system on this timeframe.

A lot of false signals are filtered out of this system compared to the long-term single moving average systems and the previous system examples. This system produced good returns by doubling capital, even as the market was sideways for 15 years. This is the best system tested in long-term, sideways market environments. This system was flat for a long time, like the QQQ ETF price itself, but it caught large uptrends early, while the ETF price and returns remained flat over the long-term. It is referred to as the Silver Cross.

Here are the variables that this platform uses to help understand any variance against other back testing sites or software. These were my settings.

~Dividends are included in the back tests.

~You will enter this system on the first day that the 50-day EMA crosses back over the 100-day EMA. The following back tests are based on the first cross. Back test will wait until the ETF crosses above the moving average before making the first buy. This system waits for a better trend signal to enter after a 50-day/100-day EMA crossover. This is not a system to enter immediately, because the results will be skewed with an initial bad risk/reward entry at elevated levels if the moving averages are already crossed.

~This system's signals are taken at the end of the day, the day of the actual moving average crossover. This is the daily chart timeframe. It looks to enter or exit at the end of the day based on whether the 50-day EMA is over or under the 100-day EMA. It only gives a signal at this crossover, and this system may go weeks and months with no entry or exit signals. You will be in cash when the 50-day EMA is below the 100-day EMA, and long when the 50-day EMA is above the 100-day EMA.

~This is a moving average crossover system, not a moving average system.

~You are trading a moving average crossing another moving average instead of price crossing a moving average.

~This system will keep you long through strong bull markets.

~This system will likely take you to cash as a market starts to trend downward.

~This system will help you avoid the large pullbacks, bear markets, and crashes.

~This system uses the 50-day exponential moving average and the 100-day exponential moving average. This 50-day and 100-day moving averages of prices is based on the total return data series that includes dividends and distributions with more weight given to the more current prices.

~The 50-day exponential moving average is the average of 50 daily total return values with more weight given to the more current prices.

~The 100-day exponential moving average is the average of 100 daily total return values with more weight given to the more current prices.

~This system is taking a signal only when the 50-day EMA moves through the 100-day EMA on the daily timeframe. This system attempts to balance the risk of giving back capital gains during a bull market with staying long when an uptrend is confirmed. However, this option helps performance by reducing the time frame of the long-term moving average signal to reduce the wait time for the 50-

day EMA to move all the way back to the 200-day crossover to just the 100-day EMA.

~This system generally gets you out faster than the 250-day SMA or the 200-day EMA system, daily.

~This system can get you back in quicker if the market rallies strong on the daily chart versus the 250-day SMA or a 200-day EMA.

~This system is watched if a 50-day/100-day moving average cross is about to happen.

~This system gives you a faster long-term moving average line with the 100-day EMA versus the 200-day EMA. This system should have quicker exits to lock in profits, and quicker entries over the long-term.

How would the 50-day EMA/100-day EMA Crossover System perform?

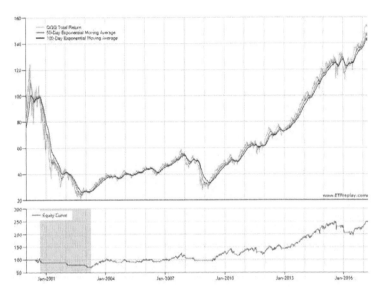

Chart Courtesy of ETFreplay.com

Historical 16 year backtest				
Backtest period	January 3rd 2000 to March 24th 2017			

Backtest Parameters — **50 day/100 day EMA price crossover**

Winning Trades	Losing Trades		Median Win	Median Loss
52.9%	47.1%		13.56%	-8.01%

Maximum Consecutive Trades			Average Days in a Trade	
Wins	Losses		Wins	Losses
3	4		297	30

Max Drawdown			Return percentage	
Backtest	$QQQ		Backtest	$QQQ
-35.4%	-83%		149.0%	48.90%

Historical backtest in a sideways market				
Backtest period	March 24 2000 to June 18 2015			

Backtest Parameters — **50 day/100 day EMA price crossover**

Winning Trades	Losing Trades		Median Win	Median Loss
53.3%	46.7%		12.60%	-7.73%

Maximum Consecutive Trades			Average Days in a Trade	
Wins	Losses		Wins	Losses
3	4		297	27

Max Drawdown			Return percentage	
Backtest	$QQQ		Backtest	$QQQ
-35.4%	-83.0%		144.0%	23.5%

Historical backtest from a market top to a market bottom				
Backtest period	March 24 2000 to October 10 2002			

Backtest Parameters — **50 day/100 day EMA price crossover**

Winning Trades	Losing Trades		Median Win	Median Loss
0.0%	100.0%		0.00%	-11.09%

Maximum Consecutive Trades			Average Days in a Trade	
Wins	Losses		Wins	Losses
0	2		0	46

Max Drawdown			Return percentage	
Backtest	$QQQ		Backtest	$QQQ
-24.8%	-83.0%		-20.9%	78.4%

Back test data courtesy of ETFreplay.com

The 10-day/ 200-day Exponential Moving Average Crossover System

This system uses the fast 10-day EMA filtering the long-term 200-day EMA. These are two of the best trend filters on their own timeframe, and combined they are the best trend trading system versus buying and holding the QQQ ETF that we've tested. This system cuts the drawdown by about two-thirds, and more than triples the return of the ETF. While the winning percentage is low, the results are good. The returns are good long-term, especially considering the small drawdowns. This is a good trend trading system that easily beats buy and hold.

Here are the variables that this platform uses to help understand any variance against other back testing sites or software. These were my settings.

~Dividends are included in the back tests.
~You will enter this system on the first day that the 10-day EMA crosses back over the 200-day EMA. The following back tests are based on the first cross. Back test will wait until the ETF crosses above the moving average before making the first buy. This system waits for a trend signal to enter after a 10-day/200-day EMA crossover. This is not a

system to enter immediately, because the results will be skewed with an initial bad risk/reward entry at elevated levels if the moving averages are already crossed.

~This system's signals are taken at the end of the day, the day of the actual moving average crossover. This is the daily chart timeframe and it is a long-term system, only looking to enter or exit at the end of the day based on whether the 10-day EMA is over or under the 200-day EMA. It only gives a signal at this crossover, and this system can go weeks and months with no entry or exit signals. You will be in cash when the 10-day EMA is below the 200-day ~EMA and long when the 10-day EMA is above the 200-day EMA.

~This is a moving average crossover system not the standard moving average system.

~You are trading a moving average crossing another moving average instead of price crossing a moving average.

~This system will keep you long through strong bull markets.

~This system will likely take you to cash as the market starts to trend downward.

~This system helps you avoid the large pullbacks, bear markets, and crashes.

~This system uses the 10-day exponential moving average and the 200-day exponential moving average. This 10-day and 200-day moving averages of prices is based on the total return data series that includes dividends and distributions and gives more weight to the more current price action.

~An exponential moving average (EMA) is a type of moving average that is like a simple moving average, except that more weight is given to the latest data.

~The 200-day exponential moving average is the average of 200 daily total return values with more wait given to near term prices.

~The 10-day exponential moving average is the average of 20 daily total return values with more weight given to the more current prices.

~This system takes a signal only when the 10-day EMA moves through the 200-day EMA on the daily timeframe. This system attempts to balance the risk of giving back capital gains during a fast pullback in a bull market, while staying long when an uptrend is quickly confirmed. However, this system option helps with faster signals than the long-term single moving average systems.

~The 10-day/200-day EMA crossover system delays your entry from when price crosses over the 200-day or 250-day moving averages. This helps avoid false signals and some volatility. Not only must the price go back over long-term moving averages, but the short-term moving average must also go back over the long-term moving average.

~This system is only watched at the end of the day when a 10-day/200-day moving average cross is about to happen.

~The 10-day EMA is your signal line, filtering long-term systems like the 200-day EMA and 250-day SMA.

How would the 10-day EMA /200-day EMA perform?

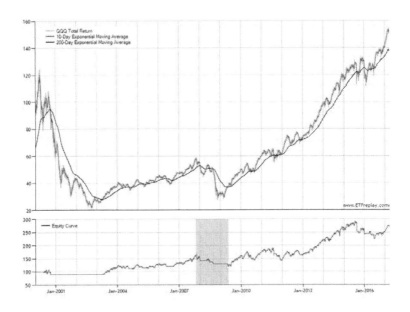

Chart Courtesy of ETFreplay.com

Historical 16 year backtest					
Backtest period	January 3rd 2000 to March 24th 2017				
Backtest Parameters			10 day/200 day EMA price crossover		

Winning Trades	Losing Trades		Median Win	Median Loss
39.1%	60.9%		18.33%	-3.65%

Maximum Consecutive Trades			Average Days in a Trade	
Wins	Losses		Wins	Losses
3	5		293	25

Max Drawdown			Return percentage	
Backtest	$QQQ		Backtest	$QQQ
-27.6%	83.0%		173.8%	55.3%

Historical backtest in a sideways market					
Backtest period	March 24 2000 to June 18 2015				
Backtest Parameters			10 day/200 day EMA price crossover		

Winning Trades	Losing Trades		Median Win	Median Loss
47.1%	52.9%		17.65%	-4.51%

Maximum Consecutive Trades			Average Days in a Trade	
Wins	Losses		Wins	Losses
3	4		301	26

Max Drawdown			Return percentage	
Backtest	$QQQ		Backtest	$QQQ
-27.6%	-83.0%		184.2%	28.8%

Historical backtest from a market top to a market bottom					
Backtest period	March 24 2000 to October 10 2002				
Backtest Parameters			10 day/200 day EMA price crossover		

Winning Trades	Losing Trades		Median Win	Median Loss
0.0%	100.0%		0.00%	-10.94%

Maximum Consecutive Trades			Average Days in a Trade	
Wins	Losses		Wins	Losses
0	1		0	85

Max Drawdown			Return percentage	
Backtest	$QQQ		Backtest	$QQQ
-18.8%	83.0%		-10.9%	-77.5%

Back test data courtesy of ETFreplay.com

The 200-day Exponential Moving Average Crossover System

Here is the quickest, easiest way to beat buy and hold investing. By using a moving average as a price filter, you can easily exit before a correction, crash, or bear market and enter again at the first sign of a recovery. With a quantified moving average, you can capture large winning trades and limit the size of your losses. You can stay on the right side of the long-term trend when the sky is the limit, and lock in profits and go to cash when the sky starts to fall. The magic of this system isn't in this one line, rather it's in the asymmetry that creates unlimited upside profits while capping losses. It's a long-term winner.

Here are the variables that this platform uses to help understand any variance against other back testing sites or software. These were my settings for this first back test.

~Dividends are included in the back tests.
~You will enter this system the first time that price crosses back up over the 200-day EMA. The following back tests are based on the first cross. Back test will wait until ETF

crosses above the moving average before making the first buy. This system waits for a better risk/reward ratio to enter at a break back over the 200-day EMA. This is not a system to enter immediately and take a position on the first day of trading, because the results will be skewed with an initial bad risk/reward entry at elevated levels. You must wait for a daily crossover and close over the 200-day EMA.

~This system's signals are taken at the end of day. This is a long-term system, only looking to enter or exit at the end of the day when price has crossed over or under the 200-day EMA. This system has potential to go for months and even a year with no signal. During downtrends in a bear market when the 200-day EMA is not retaken, it keeps you safely in cash.

~This was the 200-day exponential moving average used. The moving average is based on the total return data series that includes dividends and distributions.

~An exponential moving average (EMA) is a type of moving average that is like a simple moving average, except that more weight is given to the latest data.

~The 200-day moving average is the average of 200 daily total return values with more wait given to near term prices.

~This system will take less signals than the short-term moving average systems in this book. It means accepting more risk of giving back open profits, but you can capture a long-term trend with less noise and shake outs. However, this long-term moving average option helps you compare it with the other systems in the book, so you can decide if this additional risk of giving back open profits is better than being subjected to more frequent false signals during volatile price action.

How Does the 200-day EMA Perform as an End of Day Trading Signal?

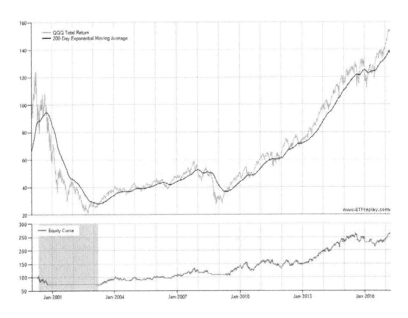

Chart courtesy of ETF Replay

Historical 16 year backtest

Backtest period   January 3rd 2000 to March 24th 2017

Backtest Parameters			**200 day EMA price crossover**	

Winning Trades	Losing Trades		Median Win	Median Loss
27.4%	72.6%		5.53%	-1.55%

Maximum Consecutive Trades			Average Days in a Trade	
Wins	Losses		Wins	Losses
3	10		150	9

Max Drawdown			Return percentage	
Backtest	$QQQ		Backtest	$QQQ
-33.7%	-83.0%		161.0%	62.2%

Historical backtest in a sideways market

Backtest period   March 24 2000 to June 18 2015

Backtest Parameters			**200 day EMA price crossover**	

Winning Trades	Losing Trades		Median Win	Median Loss
29.4%	70.6%		5.53%	-1.84%

Maximum Consecutive Trades			Average Days in a Trade	
Wins	Losses		Wins	Losses
3	10		153	9

Max Drawdown			Return percentage	
Backtest	$QQQ		Backtest	$QQQ
-33.7%	-83.0%		155.4%	34.6%

Historical backtest from a market top to a market bottom

Backtest period   March 24 2000 to October 10 2002

Backtest Parameters			**200 day EMA price crossover**	

Winning Trades	Losing Trades		Median Win	Median Loss
0.0%	100.0%		0.00%	-3.07%

Maximum Consecutive Trades			Average Days in a Trade	
Wins	Losses		Wins	Losses
0	8		0	13

Max Drawdown			Return percentage	
Backtest	$QQQ		Backtest	$QQQ
-31.8%	-83.0%		-27.2%	-76.5%

Back test data courtesy of ETFreplay.com

The 250-day Simple Moving Average Crossover System

What is the simplest way to make money in the stock market? Buying with a large safety margin maximizes your potential for profits. While this signal is rare, it can keep you in the market for a year or more as price trends far from your entry. Moving averages themselves change, so this system works when the 250-day SMA has become higher when the exit happens. If price did plunge, this system would take you out before a large downtrend. If it's a false signal, the system gets you back in as price moves back over the 250-day SMA.

Getting in at the beginning of an uptrend immediately after a downtrend presents the best risk/reward ratio for maximum gains. This is the best performing system in this book. This is the signal that likely triggers after a market meltdowns, and the first indication that the market may be done going down. This is the answer to the question of where to get back in after you get out during a market crash or panic.

Here are the variables that this platform uses to help understand any variance against other back testing sites or software. These were my settings.

~Dividends are included in the back tests.

~You will enter this system on the first day that price crosses back up over the 250-day SMA at the end of that trading day. The following back tests are based on the first cross. Back test will wait until the ETF crosses above the moving average before making the first buy. This system waits for a better risk/reward ratio to enter at a break back over the 250-day SMA. This is not a system to enter immediately, because the results will be skewed with an initial bad risk/reward entry at elevated levels. You must wait for a daily price crossover of the 250-day SMA before making your first buy. This will likely cause you to wait for a pullback in the market, with price already above the 250-day SMA, except during corrections and bear markets.

~This system's signals are taken at the end of the day, the same day of the actual cross. This is the daily chart timeframe and it is a long-term system, only looking to enter or exit at the end of the day based on whether price is over or under the 250-day SMA. It only gives a signal at that cross and this system can go months and even a year with no entry or exit signals. You will be in cash when price is below the 250-day SMA and long when price is above the 250-day SMA.

~This system will keep you long through bull markets.

~This system will likely take you to cash as a market starts to go into a correction.

~This system helps you avoid the worst part of bear markets and crashes.

~This was the 250-day simple moving average used. This 250-day moving average of prices is based on the total return data series that includes dividends and distributions.

~The simple moving average is the average (arithmetic mean) of the specified number of data points.

~The 250-day moving average is the average of 250 daily total return values

~This second system is taking a signal only when price moves through the 250-day simple moving average on the daily timeframe. This system means accepting more capital gains forfeiture risk during a bull market because you're waiting until the 250-day SMA is crossed instead of just the 200-day SMA. However, this second option helps to avoid the noise of moves through the 200-day moving average that are false.

~This system gets you out faster daily than the month end system, and helps avoid any sharp, monthly moves.

~This system is the slowest in this book, but it will get you back in quicker if the market rallies strong on the daily chart versus using a monthly system.

~This is a very slow system, and you only need to watch if price is close to the 250-day moving average. It will keep you long with the buy and hold investors during uptrends in the market.

~The drawback of this system is that you could take many signals back and forth and lose money when price is near the 250-day SMA if the price range is volatile. This system is only effective in markets that are tightly rangebound, trading around the 250-day SMA.

How Does the 250-day SMA Perform as an End of Day Trading Signal?

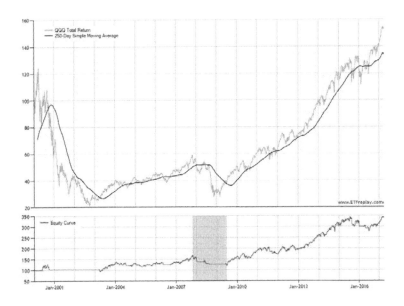

Chart Courtesy of ETFreplay.com

Historical 16 year backtest					
Backtest period	January 3rd 2000 to March 24th 2017				
Backtest Parameters			**250 day SMA price crossover**		

Winning Trades	Losing Trades		Median Win	Median Loss
24%	76%		16.25%	-1.32%

Maximum Consecutive Trades			Average Days in a Trade	
Wins	Losses		Wins	Losses
2	9		224	9

Max Drawdown			Return percentage	
Backtest	$QQQ		Backtest	$QQQ
-23.7%	-83.0%		218.9%	82.9%

Historical backtest in a sideways market				
Backtest period	March 24 2000 to June 18 2015			
Backtest Parameters			**250 day SMA price crossover**	

Winning Trades	Losing Trades		Median Win	Median Loss
25.6%	74.4%		16.25%	-1.65%

Maximum Consecutive Trades			Average Days in a Trade	
Wins	Losses		Wins	Losses
2	9		240	9

Max Drawdown			Return percentage	
Backtest	$QQQ		Backtest	$QQQ
-23.7%	-83.0%		212.7%	51.7%

Historical backtest from a market top to a market bottom				
Backtest period	March 24 2000 to October 10 2002			
Backtest Parameters			**250 day SMA price crossover**	

Winning Trades	Losing Trades		Median Win	Median Loss
0.0%	100.0%		0.00%	-2.55%

Maximum Consecutive Trades			Average Days in a Trade	
Wins	Losses		Wins	Losses
0	3		0	30

Max Drawdown			Return percentage	
Backtest	$QQQ		Backtest	$QQQ
-22.3%	-83.0%		-8.9%	-73.5%

Back test data courtesy of ETFreplay.com

Risk Management

You must base your QQQ ETF position sizing on two things. How much you want to lose on any single trade, and the maximum drawdown in account capital you are willing to accept. The maximum loss for a single losing trade for the systems in this book is about 10% from entry to stop loss. Some are slightly more, but most are much less. For the next example, we will use 10% loss in an individual trade.

If you never want to lose more than 1% on any one trade and you are trading with a $100,000 account, you don't want to lose more than $1,000 in a single losing trade from entry to exit. The stop loss level is the price level where you get the crossover exit signal. We work back to position sizing at the entry. If you enter a trade based on the entry signal of the crossover and put 100% of your trading capital in the trade, then the percentage size of your loss will reflect in your total account.

Many of the losses in this book are 5% from the entry price. if you are long 100% of your capital, a 5% loss in any single trade will be a 5% loss for your total account balance. One losing trade of 5% for the underlying QQQ in a single trade would also equal a 5% drawdown in your full account when you go all in on a single trade. The maximum drawdown shown in each system back test would also reflect on the full drawdown in your account.

Examples based on a 5% loss on a single trade entry on exit:

(Example: You enter at $100 and exit with a stop loss at $95).

~A 100% position size of your total trading capital gives you a potential 5% loss on your total trading capital. If the system's maximum drawdown is 30%, then your total trading capital would be a 30% drawdown.

~A 50% position size of your total trading capital gives you a potential 2.5% loss on your total trading capital with a 5% single trade loss. If the system's maximum drawdown is 30%, then your total trading capital would be a 15% drawdown.

~A 25% position size of your total trading capital gives you a potential 1.25% loss on your total trading capital with a 5% single trade loss. If the system's maximum drawdown is 30%, then your total trading capital would be a 7.5% drawdown.

~A 20% position size of your total trading capital gives you a potential 1% loss on your total trading capital with a 5% single trade loss. If the system's maximum drawdown is 30%, then your total trading capital would be a 6% drawdown.

~A 10% position size of your total trading capital gives you a potential 0.5% loss on your total trading capital with a 5% single trade loss. If the system's maximum drawdown is 30%, then your total trading capital would be a 3% drawdown.

The signals in this book are just the technical part of a trading system. Signals tell you when to get in and where to get out of a trade. These are basic trend following signals, and you must add your own position sizing parameters inside your own system of diversified. For investors that only hold positions in the stock market, these systems and the QQQ ETF is a great way to get tech exposure inside your 401K or IRA retirement account.

For investors, this is a safer way to get tech exposure than buy and hold.

I believe the QQQ ETF if a great trading and investment vehicle, and has a place in both investor's portfolios and trend trading systems. The size of your position and risk exposure is an individual decision that each of us must make based on our financial goals, time frame, risk tolerance, and portfolio construction.

Reality Check

The moving average systems in this book are not meant to be the end-all of trading and investing. They are the basic principles of trend following systems and are meant to give an alternative to buy and hold investments in the tech sector. The tech sector tends to be the most volatile and cyclical, with an increased chance that an individual stock will crash when they lose their edge or face new competitors. The tech sector has the most potential for both large wins and big losses. It's critical that you have a solid, well-tested plan for exit and entry.

The systems covered in this book are all long biased, and they perform best during strong tech bull markets, rallies, and uptrends to capture profits. These systems take you back to a cash position as the market loses momentum, and can help you get in quickly when the trend reverses.

These are long side only systems because the short side is much more difficult to trade with this more systematic, trend following approach. There is really no comparison in looking at a short side system versus a long side system in the tech sector over any long-term period. For a tech index of stocks, the long side is the way to go. Save short selling systems for individual tech stocks that are being disrupted by new competitors. While the QQQ will change its holdings and eventually always come back, the same can't be said for individual tech stocks.

The big cap tech stocks in the QQQ ETF holdings are backed by teams of people that want to see the company succeed. Big cap tech stocks are hedged with real people, sales, products, and companies with skin in the game. This creates the long-term long bias. The QQQ is designed to have a winner's bias, by keeping the winning companies inside the index and pushing the losers out early. The demand for big cap tech stocks is always present thanks to mutual funds, hedge funds, 401Ks, IRAs, and investors always in need of fresh inventory. While commodity prices are due to supply and demand, tech stocks are backed by the management of a company.

I chose the QQQ ETF for the back test models in this book because the index will survive long-term and go through cycles of accumulation and distribution. And unlike individual stocks, won't be taken down by technological advancement or changes in the economy.

I advise going to cash in this book during stock market downtrends since these system examples are not true diversified trend following systems that include the long and short side of equities, bonds, commodities, currencies, and interest rates. The QQQ ETF is not diversified outside the equities. It is a 100% stock market investment, primarily in the tech sector. These examples are intended to show the potential of beating buy and hold with these systems in the QQQ ETF.

These moving average systems were tested over a 16-year period. These examples captured the beginning and end of bull market bubbles, bear markets, sideways markets, and market crashes. I believe they are a good sample of how they work through multiple market environments.
The largest gains in these systems were from 1995-1999, which are not shown in this book. This was meant to show the robustness of systems to keep your Dot Com bubble wins with a quantified exit strategy, and continue to make money through the 2008 crash and beyond.

The annual returns of these systems closely reflect the limitations of the QQQ returns over the past 16 years. Many of these systems have good average annual returns, but are not as good on an annualized basis due to periods of flat returns that limited compounding. The returns of these systems reflect the returns of the stock market in general. That is why trend followers have diversified trend following systems so they can expose their trading system to multiple markets.

A back test is not predictive and it is not perfect. It is a historical sample of how price action behaved in the past. The future hasn't happened yet, so our tools for trading successfully must include proper risk management, a valid trading system, and the discipline to follow our chosen methodology. There is nothing magical about these moving average systems. You may find better ones, and if you do, please let me know!

The Keys to Moving Average Success

~They are on long enough time frames to avoid getting excessive entry and exit signals. Too short of a timeframe can show too many signals, causing losses by getting out too soon and getting back in too late. Overtrading can also lead to high commission costs. These systems are low frequency, ignoring intra-day volatility by only trading at the end of the day and only when an entry or exit signal is given.

~You can choose the timeframe you are most comfortable with, and the returns and drawdowns can help you decide which system is best for your personality and individual needs.

~If an exit signal is false and the market rallies, these moving average systems are all on time frames that should get you back in to catch an upswing.

~These systems get you in on the first cross signal so that you enter with a good risk/reward, rather than entering immediately or randomly.

~If you make changes to your system, parameters need to be back tested for validity through multiple market environments and then the new parameters must be followed going forward.

~Back tests are not predictions of the future or guarantees of future performance they are simply what happened with specific moving average signals during past historical price action. The odds are that patterns repeat themselves because people's emotional reactions repeat over time to create trends.

~We choose our system, position size, and markets to trade, the market will choose our returns.

Things That a Back Test Can't Illustrate:

~How it feels when real money is at risk.

~How losses feel during a downtrend.

~Your emotional stress during volatility and false signals.

~The perseverance needed to stick to a good system long-term.

~The patience to do nothing except wait for a signal.

~The temptation to optimize your mechanical system in real-time.

~The cost of taxes on your capital gains.

~The cost of commissions when you have many signals to execute.

~The liquidity of a market. (This will not be an issue with popular ETFs and indexes).

~The ability to follow entry and exit signals regardless of emotions.

~Whether it will work in the future. These are back tests on historical data, not front tests on the future.

Want to Learn More?

Try one of our step-by-step eCourses and you'll get:

-High quality videos covering trading in depth

-Real trade examples with annotated charts

-An active member community

Sign up at: http://www.newtraderu.com/moving-averages-101-signup/

Did you enjoy this book?

Please consider writing a review.

Be sure to listen to many of our titles on Audible!

Read more of our bestselling titles:

Moving Averages 101

So You Want to be a Trader

New Trader 101

Moving Averages 101

Buy Signals and Sell Signals

Trading Habits

Investing Habits

Calm Trader

Printed in Great Britain
by Amazon